Middle Child

A memoir

By Antoine Kincaid

Dedication

This memoir is a reminder of my associates, peers, friends, family, my ups and my downs, my wins and my losses, my journey throughout life, those who helped me or not so much along the way, and all the tid bits of energy, attitudes, events, incidents, spoken words, actions and circumstances molded together to make me the man that I've become.

Keeping these things in mind, this dedication is to any reader suffering, struggling, thinking about where to start, or how to keep going who may pick up this book and find at least an ounce of encouragement to just go, do, and become because you can.

Also, a dedication to myself for maintaining the perseverance and strength to keep going, when there were times I wasn't sure if I should or could. In this journey called life, I've lived, I've learned, I've survived, and I'm here forever grateful and anxiously awaiting the next chapter to come out significantly better than I started.

**I Smile to Keep from Crying,
I Cry to Keep from Smiling**

Middle Child

a memoir

MEMORIES

Middle child syndrome is one's belief that they are mostly excluded, ignored, or even outright neglected because they were born as the middle child. The middle child characteristically feels overshadowed by the older and younger siblings. The older sibling in this case is outgoing, smart, beautiful, and independent. While the younger sibling has the same characteristics, me as the middle child has the same characteristics as well. For whatever reason, I have always had that feeling of being overshadowed. Being the middle child sometimes feels like I am being left out. This is my story.....

I remember when my sister first moved to East Texas with our grandparents. Before downsizing, we lived in a three-bedroom apartment. My brother and I had bunkbeds, sharing a room. When he came from his dad's house to stay the night, he would sleep on the top bunk. We also had a basement which we used as a play area for games like hide-and-go-seek when our friends came over.

After downsizing, we went from a three-bedroom to a two-bedroom. We didn't call a

U-Haul truck because my mother was dating somebody with a car at the time. Piece by piece, we placed all the furniture inside the trunk of the car. My mother walked behind the vehicle to make sure that the furniture didn't fall out of the trunk while hitting speed bumps as we took multiple trips back and forth to our new place.

I got tired of taking all those trips, but my mother was very determined to make things happen. My mother...she is unbelievably beautiful. Her smile showed her pearly white teeth that could have easily landed her a spot on a toothpaste commercial. She was a track star when she was in high school; you can tell by looking at her calf muscles that her legs were the strongest part of her body.

She was about 5'2 and easily 100 pounds. She was a very hard-working woman. She was smart, generous, and a very fast talker who was always willing to help someone else get back on their feet. When I was growing up in Michigan, I had so many memories ... but we'll get to that in a minute.

Let me start by saying this....I wasn't the best

kid out there. Hell, I was kind of a problem child at times. Leave it to me, the middle child, to cause a big commotion over small stuff. I still remember everything that used to happen like it was just last week.

Man, I hated getting into trouble. My mom would get mad and whoop my ass like there was no tomorrow. She used to put my head in between her legs and go to work. I genuinely believe that I was the only child that got the most whoopings, while seemingly my sister and brother could get away with murder.

I do recall one day when my brother, sister, and I were downstairs hiding cards from each other. One of us put the card inside this wine glass that my mother had inside the China cabinet. I do not remember *who* broke the glass, but it pissed our mother off. She didn't ask questions. All three of us got whoopings that day. I believe I got it the worst. Damn, being the middle child sucks.

Our childhood was... simple. We didn't want much; it wasn't many crazy things that were happening back when I was growing up. If it was something going on, you didn't hear about it until a week or two later because we didn't have the internet to look things up. It wasn't like the social media we have in today's society. Half the children nowadays have smartphones, so social media is right at their fingertips. Not back then.

Although the internet was around, we didn't have access in my household. We didn't even have cable or a house phone half the time. Hell, we really couldn't afford the *wants* back when I was growing up. My mother didn't have a car, so we had to walk everywhere, catch the bus, or ask family and friends for a ride. I did not know we were poor. That didn't hit me until later in life. Honestly, we spent most of our time outside enjoying life in the cornfields or inside the basement playing games, so the lack of internet didn't mean much.

I don't know about my siblings, but all I know is when a streetlight came on, I better have my little ass in the house—either that or being in the front yard where Mama could see me through the window. There was no in-between. I was either supposed to be in the front yard playing with my friends or on my way inside the house.

Mama's house was a lot of fun. The area we lived in was divided into two neighborhoods. Our neighborhood was a bunch of apartments connected to other apartments. You could literally get into another person's apartment by going through the attic. The other neighborhood was a single-family home housing development. In the middle of the two neighborhoods was the school that everyone within that district attended. Also, in the middle of my neighborhood were these big hills that we used to slide down in the wintertime on sleds. I don't remember where we got the sleds from to slide down the hills in the wintertime once the snow started.

Now, the hills weren't the only thing I looked forward to in the winter. I also started making my money around that time by going around the neighborhood with my shovel and asking if I could get the snow off the sidewalk for $2 -$3. Sounds like it wasn't much, but it was a good way to make a little extra money, other than taking soda bottles to the grocery store to cash in for 10 cents.

On the weekends, we used to catch the bus to go to the mall and the movies. Afterward, I would go to my favorite burger place to buy a cheeseburger, fries, and a drink for about $3. Man, I still enjoy this same burger place and meal today. It was not that expensive to enjoy life as a child years ago.

As you probably guessed, my mother had three beautiful children: my brother, my sister, and myself. My sister is the intelligent one. She's a fast talker, just like Mama, but she says I was just listening slow. She's that ugly duckling that turned into a beautiful swan (I'm the only person that can talk about her). As kids, she was like a dusty, dark, ugly child. Hell, I did not know she was ugly until one day we were looking at our old school pictures. She pointed out how ugly she was back then, so I ran with it.

Our relationship is incredibly unique. We have that brother and sister bond, but I also depended on her a lot to keep things in order at home while Mama worked. She would often make sure I ate and my homework was completed.

I'll say this.... I would not be her friend if she were not my sister because she is *mean*. We would get into fights as little children all the time. She would even put her hands inside my mouth and pull my jaws apart. When I tell you that shit would hurt like hell... She would have me in tears. I wish y'all could have seen my face and felt my pain.

Unfortunately, I could not put my hands on her because she was a female. That is one thing Mama taught us brothers; never put our hands on a female no matter how bad it got.

My sister tricked me this one particular night and told me that she would help me clean out the bathtub. The deal was that she'd take her bath first, and I would use her same bathwater to take a bath in.... NASTY. Once I was done, then she would help me clean the tub out. For some reason, I thought this was a good idea. Well, we used her same bathwater, but she didn't help me clean the tub out. She got me good that day, and I didn't lay a finger on her.

On the other hand, I am smart, intelligent, determined just like Mama, with all the characteristics of middle child syndrome. I am indecisive, commonly second-guessing myself, a jokester, nonchalant attitude at times, always putting others before myself, laidback, chubby kid, and lastly extremely handsome. I had trouble in school from time to time and was eventually diagnosed with dyslexia explaining my struggles.

Then, there is the baby boy, Mr. Know It All. He knows everything about nothing, but you cannot tell him that. He knows the facts and stats about things I have no interest in. The only stats that I care about are sports; he be on some other shit. His real talent is he works very well with his hands.

He's also smart and determined like Mama because he can get anything done that he sets his mind to. We all have different personalities, which might be because we all came from the same woman but have different fathers. In fact, our brother didn't live with us. He stayed with his father and grandmother on the other side of the city. When he came over to stay the night, he slept on the top bunk, and we would talk for hours every night like little school girls. Yeah...life was pretty good.

***

My brother was pretty damn smart, my sister was smart, but for some damn reason, back then, I felt like the smart gene skipped right over me. I had to work extra hard in school. My brother and sister are outgoing and outspoken. I, on the other hand, am shy. I have to warm up around you before I open up to you. As a result, I tend to stay to myself a lot.

***

I didn't know that we were poor and required financial assistance. All I knew was that we didn't have a lot of the stuff that the other kids had. When we were growing up, my mother didn't have a car. We got around; it just took us a little longer because we had to coordinate with different people to get a ride to go here and there. We struggled, but my mother showed us a lot of love and respect for her three children.

The best Christmas that I ever had was when my mother bought us a bunch of board games. We put up a Christmas tree that year, and my little brother put the ornament up on top.

It was a great experience. We had so many gifts up under the tree, and we played board games for days after. We were spending that quality time together. It was the first Christmas where all four of us were together with a whole lot of presents under the tree.

***

My seventh-grade year was very eventful. Fun times and bad times. What can I say? I was enjoying my life. I was suspended from school more than I was in school. How I passed the seventh-grade still amazes me to this day when I look back and reminisce. Honestly, all of middle school, in general, was a joke to me. I didn't take it seriously at all. I would turn in my assignments late or wait until I got on the school bus to start doing my homework. Half the time, I wouldn't turn in my assignments at all. The only reason I passed the seventh grade was because of the leave no child behind program.

One of the classes I remember skating through was choir. It was an elective, so of course, I didn't take it seriously. I remember we had a concert one day, and instead of waiting around for it to start, I left school and walked to my auntie's and uncle's house.

I thought I could take a quick nap and chill out before the concert started. I didn't set the alarm clock, so I wounded up missing the concert. The choir director let me know that I would get five E's because that is what that assignment was worth. You know what, though? I didn't really care. That's one of several instances where I really just did whatever I wanted to do. Like I said, middle school was a damn joke.

When I wasn't at school, I was getting into something at the house. My mother worked at night, so I was basically home alone and didn't have anyone to check up on me while she was at work. In case you're wondering where my sister was and why she wasn't watching me, she was back and forth between here and my grandparent's place in Texas.

I'll tell you more about that in a sec. Now, back to life in Michigan. I would be coming in the house from school, and she'll be going to work. She would tell me to make sure to knock out all my homework before I did anything and be in the house when the street light came on.

The funny thing is she wasn't around, so she just took my word for it. Instead of doing my homework and being in the house, I was too busy trying to run the streets. I was trying to be a so-called gang member so bad. You know how it is when your parents aren't around, and you just need somewhere to fit in.

It was a group of us who used to hang out all the time. Redd, he was my homie. We were definitely the closest of the group and was always getting into some shit. I love my boy, but he was a little on the chunky side. Every time we played ball with the guys, he didn't do that good. Guess that's the price you pay for eating that last slice of pizza one too many times.

My mother and his mother were good friends when they were growing up, and they stayed around the corner from our apartment complex. I used to go over to Redd's house all the time. He had a basketball hoop in his basement and a video game upstairs in his room.

I remember I didn't see him for a while, and when I did, he had a cast on his leg. He told me he was upstairs in his room playing the video game when his TV fell on his leg. Isn't that the craziest shit you ever heard? When we weren't in his house playing basketball or the video game, we were outside catching grasshoppers.

Despite that craziness, my best friend was a very bright kid. He and my sister both had the opportunity to go to a school for smarter people, but my mother didn't have the transportation to get my sister back and forth. My friend, however, took advantage of the opportunity. Thankfully, that didn't keep us from hanging out.

Another one of the guys in the group was Max. Max was the calm, cool person of the bunch. He was the person that everyone wanted to be around. Then, you had Terry. He was a little older than us, so he was more level-headed and close to my other friend name One Time. It was a few others, but the main ones were definitely me, Redd, Max, Terry, and One Time.

It really wasn't anything to do in our little neighborhood besides play basketball and football, so we were itching to get into other habits.

I was probably the smallest one in our little group, but I had the biggest mouth because I knew that I had my friends to back me up. I will go start something knowing damn well I could not finish it. I was probably 120 pounds soaking wet with boots on. Skinny as a rail but had a whole lot of lip. Yep, I was the one always going around picking on people picking fights. Thankfully, even though I had a lot of mouth, I did not get into any real big fights at the schoolhouse.

Some of the other crazy things we would do is knock on people's doors and run away. We'd even kick in their back doors in the middle of the night and take off running. We were so reckless we would even push each other into cars to make the alarm go off. Basically, we were always looking for excitement and ways to entertain ourselves.

***

I had the opportunity of choosing between whether I wanted to live the street life. My uncle was a very hard worker, and he was all about living in the streets. On the other hand, my grandfather was also a very hard worker who lived the church life.

If we're honest, there's nothing wrong with either. Both worked hard to provide for their families, just in different ways. Now, don't get it twisted. My uncle was not killing anybody or anything like that. He was just making his money to provide for his family differently than my grandfather was.

My grandfather and I would have many conversations. He would always tell me that if a man doesn't work, he does not eat. The only man that doesn't work is a lazy man. That was the motto that he lived by.

My grandfather had me working in a concession stand, and he showed me how to make money the right way. If nothing else, working for him taught me how to save. I learned that if I wanted anything for myself, I had to work for it.

My sister, on the other hand, was the only granddaughter at the time and got whatever she wanted. We both had been playing basketball since we were in elementary school, with her only being a grade above me. I played in Buddy's—these ugly, tore up looking shoes that the poorest people use to wear—while my sister had on name brand shoes that my grandmother bought her. I didn't complain out loud, but in the back of my mind...I thought it was a bunch of bull shit.

***

Remember how I mentioned that my mother worked at night? Well, there's one particular day my mom goes to work, and one of my so-called buddies brought a BB gun over to the house. We were upstairs in my bedroom, just shooting birds and passing the time. I didn't think anything about it. I turn my back, and you'll never guess what happened. He shot a little girl in the leg with it.

Someone called the police on us, and he took off running. I didn't open the front door when the police came because I called myself being slick by using the back door to leave once I realized the cops had been called. I found out later that the police officer had left a note on the door.

I told my friends what happened and asked how I could get rid of the BB gun. Naturally, nobody had a clue, so I kept it up under my bed. I didn't get rid of the evidence. When my mother got home from work the next morning, she saw the note on the door and called the police officer back to the house. I told her it wasn't a BB gun, and I didn't have a clue on what the hell was going on. A couple minutes later, I ended up telling the truth, taking the officer upstairs to my room, and showing him where I'd hidden the BB gun. He took it, and I haven't seen it since. I didn't get a whooping, but my mother and the police officer had a serious talk with me about how serious my charges could be. I could've got in big trouble because my so-called buddy blamed everything on me. Typical.

***

Like I said before, I would start a lot of mess sometimes. Well, I remember we were at my buddies' house, and this one guy who is older and bigger than me started talking shit. We saw him around the neighborhood but didn't really know him that well.

"Man, you talk so much shit," he spat as he stepped to my face. "That's the reason why I don't like you." We immediately started fighting. I just so happened to have two of my buddies there that day. I was holding my own, but my other two buddies jumped in and broke the fight up. After that day, I would see that kid around the neighborhood every now and then. He wouldn't speak to me. It was actually kind of funny because I wanted to speak to him, but I didn't. That is until my buddies came around, then I'd talk shit. So, all this lead up to my first real ass whipping.

My first real ass-whipping was in April around Easter of my seventh-grade year. I remember talking shit to the same guy that I got into a fight with a couple of weeks earlier. This was one of those times where the guy really didn't say a whole lot, but I was just hotheaded because I had my friends with me to back me up.

This particular day, he was carrying some tacos from the taco house. I was talking shit to him, pushing him and shoving like a bully. I remember knocking the tacos out of his hands, but he still didn't fight back. Somebody came over there and told me to just leave him alone, so I backed down. It wasn't any fun if the guy wasn't fighting back anyway.

The next morning while I was waiting at the bus stop, I realized that I left my ID at the house. I knew I'd miss the bus, but I couldn't go to school without my ID. So, I had to walk home by myself without my friends. Guess who caught me on my way home? The same guy I was messing with the day before. He had a stick in one hand and a mean look on his face. I'm continuing to talk shit, and he dropped the stick, and we get to fighting one on one.

I fucked around and slipped on something, and he took advantage of my being on the ground. This kid started stumping me out right there in the middle of the sidewalk. There was nothing I could do but take each blow. He finally stopped long enough for me to run home. I swung open the door and fell on the floor.

My mother started panicking because she saw all the blood and didn't know what to do. She called the police and asked me if I wanted to press charges, and I told her no. I mean, it was just a fight. Shit like that is bound to happen. After that incident, I continued to get in trouble, so my mother made me move back to East Texas with my grandparents. It was almost like a fresh prince moment. I had to leave just so I could stay out of trouble.

***

I hated it in East Texas. It was nothing there, and I do mean nothing. Actually, I had already been there at the beginning of 6th grade and left because I didn't like it. That's when I moved back to Michigan. Then, the problems kept coming (e.g. BB gun incident and getting into that big fight), so here I was again.

Moving back to East Texas was not as bad as I thought it was going to be. Somethings didn't change at my grandparents' house. We were allowed to watch TV when my grandparents were out and about, but when they came back, everyone would scatter. You know how it is when someone turns on the lights and all the roaches would disappear? That's what it was like when our grandparents came back inside the house.

When I moved back this time around, it was more people living in the house. My auntie, uncle, and cousins had moved from

Michigan to East Texas, and everyone was living with our grandparents. It was one big happy family. The highlight of my day was going to school and hanging around the few friends I did have. I had one who played football and another who played basketball. We didn't hang out much after my 8th grade year, so I won't get into too much detail about them.

The main thing I remember is that I didn't do any schoolwork or homework, just like in Michigan. I remember joking around in the hallways and making fun of a guy named Benny who grew to become one of my best friends. He actually ended up getting held back a grade behind.

Little did I know, I was about to do the same thing. Because I didn't do my work, I failed 8th grade. Once school was out for summer, the school sent my grandparents a letter to inform them that I could go to summer school and advance to the 9th grade or repeat the 8th grade again. I did not go to summer school, so I would be right back in 8th grade.

That summer, I went to church a lot with

my grandparents in Louisiana. My sister, grandmother, and I would always go to church. My uncle was never at home when it was time to go to church. If he was, he would hide under the bed so he wouldn't have to go. That shit was so funny.

My uncle was a character. He was the type to take off all his clothes whenever he pooped and be in there all day. It literally was an all-day event for him. Most of the time, it'll be when we were about to go fishing or church.

So, once the summer ended, I was back in middle school. My second year in eighth grade, the school year did not start off so hot. I missed the first few days because we were at the park in Texas with the church. My grandfather worked at night, so when I made it home from school, I barely saw him because he'd be on his way to work. As for my grandmother, we would drive 35-45 minutes to church every single day.

Each week was the same routine. Monday was Bible study, Tuesday was basketball practice, Wednesday was Bible study, Thursday was basketball practice, and by

Friday/ Saturday was back to bible study or another basketball game. Then, of course, Sunday was for church. Sometimes we'd even go to both services.

That's all we knew as children: church, sports, and school. One person I never saw was my uncle. I do not know what he did most of the time or where he would go besides under the bed when it was time for church. On Sunday mornings, I did not see him at all.

I remember when my mother came to visit one year she didn't go to church. I didn't go to church that day either, and later on my grandma made it known that she wasn't having that. "Just because your mother here, that don't change shit," she hissed. "You still get your ass in the car on Sundays, boy."

"Yes, ma'am," I said sheepishly. I learned my lesson that day for sure. If I was at my grandparents' house, I was going to church.

If it wasn't basketball season, it was the praise team. One particular Sunday, my sister and I were riding in the car with my grandmother and she ran my foot clean over. Long story short, she thought I was all the way in the car and I wasn't. I had to go to the ER and everything. Luckily, I didn't feel any pain.

I left the ER in a day. A day or two later, I had to go back up there because the doctor had called and let me know that I had some broken toes. I had to stay off my foot for a while afterward. That was the first time that I ever had any broken bones in my body.

***

When I first went back to 8th grade the second time, I remember getting on a bus going to school and everyone asking us where we had been. I nor my sister said anything. Even the principal asked me where I was at, and I didn't tell him anything. I ran into Benny, and he instantly started laughing. "Karma's a bitch. We in the same grade again," he grinned. We kept joking around with each other the rest of the day.

That year turned out to be surprisingly good. It had its ups and downs at times. I ended up falling head over heels with this girl named PJ that stayed literally less than 200 meters away from the house. I used to call her on the weekends, and when her mother was gone, I would go over to hang out with her outside the house. She couldn't call my house.

We found out the hard way that my grandmother was mean when it came to me talking on the phone. "Antoine don't pay any bills at this house, and he's not allowed girl phone calls anyways," she'd say as she hung up in her face. That's where my sister gets her sassiness from. I always tell my sister the apple doesn't fall too far from the tree.

Even though we couldn't talk on the phone as much, we used to write letters back-and-forth to each other. Well, she used to write letters to *me*. I used to take them home and let my sister read them. Then, my sister would write them for me. It was awesome. I was crushing on a few girls when I was in eighth grade, but for some reason, PJ stuck with me for a little.

It was all fun and games til my sister, with her big mouth, told PJ's brother about us.

Her brother was in high school. He was this big dude who was the defensive end on the varsity football team. I didn't know what he'd do to me if he found out about us. Luckily, he didn't do anything, so we kept hanging out. Sadly, she ended up moving away. I do not think I dated or talk to anyone else when I was in middle school once she left.

***

Benny and I were playing basketball during gym hours all the time. I remember this coach I didn't know was always there. He saw us playing, and he pulled me off to the side and asked me if I wanted to play for the 8th grade team. I made up every excuse in the book not to play, but he was persistent. One excuse I gave him was I was failing every class. We walked around to all my teachers and he got all my grades. First lie debunked.

"What's your excuse now?" he asked sarcastically. I didn't have one. A few days later, he took me to go get a physical. He also talked to the principal and had all my classes changed so that I could be in athletics and play basketball.

Playing sports made the school year go by fast. It was fun, and it gave me a reason to do my work because I wanted to participate in games. Therefore, I had to pass all my classes with a 70 or above. You know the drill: no pass, no play. Those were the rules.

I never really played organized sports when I was living back in Michigan. I played basketball for the elementary school that I went to, but it really wasn't basketball practice because everybody from the neighborhood used to come and watch us play.

I know this one particular day, I had my sister's boots on practicing, and people were making fun of me. Somebody threw their coats onto the basketball floor and made me fall and hurt myself. They all laughed at me, and it was pretty embarrassing. Now that I was in eighth grade, it was more organized with no outsiders watching us practice.

I did not start for a while, playing my role as best I could. I do remember a few basketball games. At the beginning of the season, I was on the bench a lot; I guess the coach was trying to get a feel of the team and me since I was the new kid on the block.

One game we were down, and Coach finally called my number. He looked me in the face and said, "Bring us back." My time had finally come. I thought I was finally going to get my chance to shine.

Unfortunately, we lost that game. I don't recall by how many points, but I do remember the conversation after the game. Coach pulled me off to the side and gave me the rundown. "The reason you don't get a lot of playing time is because you're not focused on the game," he explained. "You too busy talking to the females in the stands, and you don't know what's going on."

I was pissed, but he did have a point. I was more concerned about who was in the stands than what was happening on the court.

I learned my lesson after that game. I did not travel all the way out there for no reason, so I focused more on practice and the games. It was a time when Coach had to call me inside his office because I talked about quitting. I just was not used to the structure that they had at the school, especially in the athletic department. After the few little bumps in the road, I eventually got my shit together and enjoyed basketball again.

One of the starters had a big family vacation to go to, so that is when I had the opportunity to start. It was the last game of the season, and we actually ended up winning. I had a decent game. I scored the most points and even had the most rebounds and everything. After the game, the coach came up to me and said, "Do not be afraid of your talent."

I remember the next day in school, everybody came up to me, congratulating me on a good game. That was the first time that ever happened to me. Made me feel like the big man on campus. A few weeks went by after our last basketball game, and Coach called me over the intercom to his office.

When I walked in, he had some good news. He said that he had a spot for me on the boys track team. I ran track before when I was in middle school back in Michigan. I practice a lot, but when we got to the track meet, it was not organized. Our track coach just asked us to raise our hands, and the most popular kid got chosen to run that particular event. Like I said: unorganized.

My middle school didn't have a track to practice on. Instead, we ran inside the school and did the stairs a lot. I participated for about three weeks before I stopped going to practice. I felt like it was a waste of time because we all practiced doing the same thing instead of individual events. I wasn't feeling it, so I just quit. One thing about me, I'm not afraid to call bull shit when I see it.

***

In between sports, my grandfather had chores for me to do. He liked the yard to be cut before the weekend hit so it would be fresh on Saturday. If I didn't have any homework to do or if it wasn't a varsity sport that was going on that Friday, I had to cut the grass. Saturdays, I had to wash the car for church on Sunday. Even though other males were living in the house, I felt like I was the only one that was really doing any chores.

My cousin's mother used to tell my grandfather that her children weren't doing anything, but that wasn't true for me. When my granddaddy was outside doing something, I was outside with him. He always made sure to keep me occupied by cutting down trees, burning trees, cutting the grass, washing cars....etc.

One of the styles that we had when I was going to high school in East Texas was wearing our pants with a crease. We could take off our pants, and they would be able to stand up by their selves. My uncle showed me how to iron so that I could fit in because that was the style.

Once my grandfather found out that I could iron like that, he stopped taking his clothes to the cleaners and had me ironing for him. He was paying me more than he paid the cleaners. He didn't like me asking for anything, so that was his way of putting money into my pocket. Remember the motto: I have to work for it and earn it the right way. It's funny because to this day, I still wear my pants like that with the crease in the middle. You can take them off and stand them up.

***

Anyway, my grandfather was teaching me how to be a man. He taught me that if a woman is good enough to lay up with, she is good enough to marry. We will talk about that later on. Let's get back on track right quick because there's a few things I forgot to mention.

Coach thought it was a good idea for me to run the 100-meter dash, the 4 x 100 m relay, and surprisingly, the 110 hurdles. I wasn't coordinated enough to run and jump, so I just stuck with the other two events. They turned out to be my favorites.

Part of the reason is because my uncle's best friend named Jack ran those two events and boy was he fast. I have never seen anything like it in my life besides watching it on TV. When any of my friends talked about sports, I would always bring up Jack's name. He was faster than whoever is on your mind right now.

Jack was one of the reasons I thought it would be a good idea for me to run those events. Truthfully, I was somewhat following in his footsteps. I was always around him and going to his house. I remember my uncle and I playing a video game and just sitting around looking at all his trophies, medals, and ribbons. I knew I wanted some of those items, too, but I knew that I had to work hard to get them.

His mother was also our school bus driver. I guess she was blind or something because we would sit in the back of the bus and my uncle and his two best friends used to beat me up all the time. It wasn't anything too serious; just joking around playing and having a good time.

I can remember sometime before my last track meet in middle school I somehow managed to pull my hamstring, so I didn't practice as much. I was too busy nursing my hamstring. I do remember that the track meet was probably my worst ever. I had a pulled hamstring, our fastest person on the track team was a no-show, and we had to get another person that never practiced with us to take his place.

I don't know the conversation that he and the coach had the next day, but the look on his face wasn't a good one. Eventually, he apologized to the whole team. We forgave him easily and put it in the past. It was a lesson learned from all of us.

New Beginnings

It took me a while to recover from my hamstring injury. You name it, I did it. I heated it, shocked it, rode a bike, etc. I did everything that I could, but it just didn't heal as fast as I wanted it to.

I remember getting a new athletic director for the school. My hamstring was still hurt, but I wanted to impress the new athletic director while doing the football drills. He told me to take it easy and asked me had I ever played football before. I told him not organized football for a school, but I was going to play next year.

That summer went by quickly. I did the usual—worked at my grandparent's concession stand. My uncle was more excited about me becoming a freshman than I was because of the football season that was right around the corner.

I was *not* ready to practice football twice a day. Hell, the whole summer, I ate and did whatever I wanted. The whole time I did everything you could think of besides working out. Think about it. I worked in my grandparent's concession stand where it was nothing but snacks. What did you think would happen?

Oh, and did I mention I stayed with my grandparents, so I got spoiled all the time? My favorite dish is banana pudding and OMG. My grandmother made it on a regular. When she cooked, she would throw down, and it was never anything healthy at the table.

I don't even remember my grandmother ever making so much as a salad except when we had fried fish. Every time fish was on the menu, my grandmother would make this one dish with tomatoes, onions, a few other vegetables, some type of oil, and seasoning.

I was always outside with my grandfather doing chores, so I was barely in the kitchen. I believe the only time I was in the kitchen was to help clean up. I always thought that was a double whammy—outside doing yard work all day then having to help clean up the kitchen later on.

You might be like, "Well, someone has to do it!" True, but my sister ole lazy mean ass was always trying to boss people around and wouldn't do anything for herself. Do this... do that. Damn. What the hell *you* doing? It was always something with her. We couldn't be in the same room for more than a week without us getting into it about something. Sorry...had to rant for a moment.

I remember my friend picking me up for football practice. I was excited and nervous at the same time. The first part of practice, all the coaches introduced themselves since more than half of the staff was new. We had to write our names on some tape and stick it on our helmets so they could get to know us.

Since it was my first time ever playing football in high school, they had to find the right position for me. I ended up being running back on offense and corner back on defense. When I tell you I was out of shape, I almost died out there on that field.

After practice as we were on our way to the house, I'd lay down in the back of the truck and feel my body cramping up. My friend thought it was funny. He told me to drink some pop because it had acid my body needed and to snack on something but not eat a full meal because we had to get ready for round two.

He said he'd come to pick me up once it's time again. Great. Oh, and the nice dude who asked me if I was going to try out and play football next year for school? He turned out to be not so nice. All I remember him doing is yelling, cussing, and fussing all throughout the day.

Yeah, football was an experience that I wasn't ready for, but it was an experience that I'm glad I traveled down. I was writing a new chapter in my life.

I always wanted to play football, and it was easy to get my grandmother to agree because she had my uncle in her ear. The only thing that I had to do was ask her if I could play. I didn't know too much about football prior to playing for the school. I had played neighborhood pick-up football with my buddies, but that was it. The best time to play was in the wintertime in the snow.

It was a different feeling playing for the

school and being organized with referees and going to different schools to play. I didn't start the first half of the season, but once we got into district, that's when I had my chance because our starting running back—my best friend Kai—moved up to varsity.

That was one of the best experiences that I've ever had in my life, going to different schools and playing against different people. We had the best JV record the school had ever seen at the time. Our football team made it all the way to the big dance to the state championship game. I had the opportunity of moving up to varsity after the JV season was over with, but I chose to do basketball instead.

Looking back, that's one of the biggest regrets that I've ever had because I feel down deep inside that I made the wrong decision. I should've moved up to the varsity football team after our JV football season, but I turned it down when the coach asked.

I also turned it down a second time at the beginning of the basketball season. It was our first game in, and we were doing warm-ups when he asked me if I wanted to play. He told me that if I didn't play basketball that night, I still had the chance to move up. Well, I turned it down because I was so eager to play ball. At that time, it was my favorite sport.

The JV basketball season was very interesting. I don't remember how many basketball games we won, but my same buddy who used to pick me up for football practice also picked me up for basketball games.

He stayed right around the corner. He was real good people, and I learned a lot of different things from him. Although he played varsity football, he was on the JV basketball team with me. Honestly, our basketball skills weren't as good as our football skills. I believe in one game, we had roughly 27 turnovers between the both of us.

We both played point guard, but I couldn't dribble to my left for nothing in the world. Come to think about it, I had a hard time running the football to the left as well. I guess my left side of the brain just had a hard time functioning when it came to sports. Hell, maybe even life in general.

We only hung out at school events because I wasn't allowed to go over to his house. I always had to sneak and walk that half mile if I wanted to hang out. He was a cool kid, and he never charged me for picking me up. Even when I missed the bus, he never asked for a dime. When we had the 27 turnovers in that one basketball game, we had to do 27 suicides to make up for it. I almost died that day at practice.

I still remember in the middle of the basketball season. one of the varsity basketball players pulled me to the side and said, "You have a lot of talent. Do not be afraid to use it." I heard what he was saying, but I didn't really feel it.

We didn't win district, and I didn't have the same opportunity that I had during the football season to move up to varsity once the playoffs hit. It looked like my love for basketball was slowly fading away.

Even though sports were coming to a close, that didn't mean that school was about to be boring for me. When I tell you I was a class clown, I used to love all the attention. Since there was no more football or basketball, I got bored.

I didn't think I was going to run track, but my buddy talked me into joining the team. He said that it would be a great experience for someone my age, so I gave it a shot. I'm glad I did.

I started off on the JV track team, and the coaches could tell that it wasn't challenging for me. I was a freshman, though, so I had to start somewhere. At our district track meet, both the varsity and JV boys teams took first place in every event. I don't know what happened, but somehow, I ended up on the boy's varsity track team. After our district meet, we broke the 4 x 100 m relay record.

My second time running on the JV track team, I was the last leg. When I ran for varsity, I was the first leg. We took fourth or fifth place... I can't remember but we winded up breaking the 4 x 100 sprint relay school record. To this day, I still believe that we hold that record.

Our warm-up for the 4 x 100 sprint relay was crazy. We would do different chants to hype us up and get in the mood to run. We were not cocky, but we knew what type of talent we had when all four of us were put together.

Our second leg on the 4 x 100 sprint relay team was a beast. Not only did he do the 100 and 200, but he also did the pole vault. When you talking about somebody that's quiet, he was very soft-spoken, intelligent, and humble. He was so talented that he had the opportunity to play in the senior bowl football game. He was just a humble guy all the way around, not cocky like I was.

Our third leg was a goofy character, but he was also humble. He was a senior like the second leg and had been on the track team for years. He ran the 800-meter event and was also on the 4 x 400 relay as well. He pretty much ran the whole track practice, and if anybody else needed some help, he would help them out too.

We had a class together, and we would just be laughing and joking and having a good time. We took the same energy to track practice too. I remember one day, he pulled me off to the side during basketball season to tell me that the rest of the 4 x 100 team was already getting ready for the track season. I thought it was too early to be working out for track season, but they were dedicated.

Our last leg was laid-back. We never had any real heart to hearts or anything. He was a cool dude who drove a blue Cutlass. Honestly, he was more of a ladies' man. When we went to track meets, that's all we would talk about, females.

My freshman year, when we made it to regionals, we met the female track team from a rival high school. We kept in contact with those ladies over the next few years and even ran into them again at another track meet. It was like nothing had changed. We picked up from where we left off. We did not make it to state in the 4 x 100 that year; we got third instead. I was nervous, and I did not run a good leg. Just because the relay team had a bad meet doesn't mean the other guys didn't do well individually.

If I remember correctly, our second leg made it to state in the 100-meter, 200-meter, and pole-vault events. I regret to this day that we didn't make it to state in a 4 x 100 my freshman year because we would've won the whole thing. That still haunts me to this day like a ghost.

I made the varsity team my sophomore year. The only thing the coach told me to do was keep my grades up. This one particular track meet I remember looking around and saying we were going to smoke some guys who were in the stands. Our second leg turned around and glared at me. "Man, you don't need to say that," he said as he rolled his eyes. "Just show it. You don't have to be cocky."

After that little talk, I had a hard time giving him the stick during practice. For some reason, I just gave up. When he saw how defeated I looked, he had another quick heart to heart. "Man, you never give up," he said encouragingly. "You always fight til the last minute. If we get disqualified, you let the refs DQ us. Not you."

There was nothing I could say to that. I just took his word for it because he had been there before. I was trying to get where he was going. He had already made a name for himself, and I was trying to make a name for myself too. He was teaching me a valuable lesson that I was going to carry with me for the rest of my high school career.

Our boy's track team was focused. Almost every meet we went to somebody was breaking a record. Other schools hated when our bus would pull up to the stadium because we were so good. Once I finally got on board, we were never cocky. We came to take care of business, and we left. That year, we ended up breaking the 4 x 100 record at regionals.

Compared to my freshman year, I was more focused. I learned from my mistakes. My sophomore year wasn't as good as my freshman year when it came to playing football. I was the starting running back on the JV football team and was projected to have a lot of rushing yards that season. I was focused, and I knew what to expect.

The varsity football team just came off an awesome year and made it all the way to the big dance before falling short in the finals. We were ranked in the top 10 and everything. I also had the opportunity to work out with the varsity football team that year before the football season hit.

I was excited, but the unthinkable happened. The play that I was injured on: Pro left 37 cut back. I still remember it like it was yesterday. I'm running out of bounds, and somebody grabbed my shoulders from the back and threw me to the ground. My leg was like a pretzel. The coach said they never saw anything like it. Come to find out, I had a partially torn ACL.

My grandparents couldn't afford insurance at the time, and looking back at it, I'm glad they couldn't because I probably wouldn't be in the army today. The doctors probably would've tried to cut me open and have surgery. The military probably wouldn't have allowed me to enlist had I have had that operation.

I missed the whole JV football season. Once the playoffs hit, I was healthy enough to practice. They did let me move up to varsity during the playoff time. I still went to every JV and varsity football game while I was injured.

I was a water boy who had to "earn my meal ticket," as one of the coaches would say. They still made me feel part of the team. I didn't know that I was going to miss almost a whole season. Hell, no one did. The last game of the varsity football season before the playoffs, I thought I was going to get in the game. Coach was looking at me and told me to wait my turn. My turn never came.

My sophomore year, I made the varsity basketball team, but I was falling out of love with basketball. Instead, I was more focused on track and football. After about 3 games, I walked into the coach's office and told him I didn't want to play anymore. He wasn't thrilled, but his thought process was, "We can win with you; we can win without you.

We can lose with you; we can lose without you." He let me go easy.

I was never really good at basketball to begin with. I couldn't dribble or shoot with my left hand. Like I said earlier, it's like the left side of my brain doesn't function correctly. I picked up powerlifting to get me ready for the next season of sports.

My upper body wasn't very strong, but I could deadlift 450 pounds. I squatted somewhere around 425-430. My bench press was roughly around 185-205.

I broke 1,000 pounds in all three events one time, which I was very excited about. It was my first medal that I ever received for any sports, but I didn't take it too seriously. It was just to keep me in shape and get me better for the upcoming season.

***

I hated the holiday season with my grandparents. I believe that's why I played sports—to get out the house and have a little bit of freedom because I wasn't allowed to sleep over at any of my friends' houses. I couldn't even go visit the ones who lived down the street.

I wasn't allowed to do a lot of different things in the holiday season. Sometimes, I didn't see eye to eye with my Grandma. During Christmas, I'd go over to my auntie's house. She treated me like one of her own boys, but I was the only one who was doing chores most of the time. She would have her older son do chores, but he didn't do them correctly. If he didn't do them correctly, then I would get in trouble.

Everything seemed like it went wrong in the house when it came to chores and cleaning. She pointed the finger at *me* because I was older. The crazy thing is he didn't listen to her, so I don't know what made her think he was going to listen to me.

I remember one time the radio broke, and she blamed me. The dryer broke too from me *supposedly* putting too many clothes inside. It was always my fault because I'm the middle child.

When they stayed in Michigan, she came home and was just yelling about why this isn't cleaned up and why this isn't done. I wasn't the only one who lived there, but the finger was pointed at me every time something went wrong.

My thing was this: if you look at me as one of your sons, then why didn't I get anything when Christmas came around? Everybody got something besides me, but I was cool with it. You know, middle child stuff.

When she let me come over, she'd let me wear her son's clothes. As soon as I went home, though, I had to take them off. She had more money than my mother, so you know how that went with sibling rivalry. It was crazy because they will get into it, and I will be in the middle of a mess.

This would even happen back when we all lived in Michigan. I didn't know any better; I was just a kid. I just wanted to play and hang out with my cousins and come over to the house and play video games. My mother couldn't afford to buy me video games, so I would go over to their house.

If I wasn't at her house, I was at my cousin Big Muscle's house. One particular summer we were riding bikes, but I couldn't keep up. I was a little thing, and I wasn't as fast as them, so I rode on the handlebars for miles.

Once I got off the handlebars, my ass would hurt. I could barely walk, but I loved being around them. When they moved to Georgia, Big Muscle started doing his own thing. A lot changed once they left, so I won't say too much about them.

***

My junior year of high school, I was becoming the big man on campus because all the people who played varsity when I first started had graduated. Our head coach went off to another school, so our DB coach became the new head coach. Even with the changes, we didn't miss a beat. The talent was still there.

Evidently, our districts realigned every 2-3 years. We were pretty good as a team, but we weren't as good as we could have been. Our mindset was different from the seniors who had just graduated. They were the ones who took their team to state back to back both my freshman and my sophomore year. We still had to make a name for ourselves. The games were really physical that year. We lost both times to the same school, the Cheetahs, and one against another one.

I remember this one particular practice when the coach told me to go get my knee brace because he wanted me to start as running back. I was shocked because that spot belonged to one of my buddies.

Luckily, he was very humble about it; he didn't get mad at me. He was really helpful and picked me up when I got low during some games. He showed me nothing but love and respect—absolutely no hateful bones in his body. I appreciated that he wasn't sour about how I got the starting job over him.

I didn't play as much in the regular season, but I played a lot in district. We had an awesome regular season, but we got put out in the second round of playoffs. Like I mentioned before, we had the same talent. Our mindset was just different. Now, football season was more fun this time because I actually got to play and didn't get hurt. We didn't go as far, but we had a good time.

The football season itself was a trip. I remember right after a game, the team went to a Mexican restaurant in EastTexas. My buddy Clinton was a good boy, but this particular day he wanted to be mischievous. So, he says something crazy to one of the workers there named Brittney. He was flirting with her and trying to get her phone number, but he came at her incorrectly.

I stepped in because I didn't want anything going crazy because she didn't know his personality like I did. I sweet-talked her and ended up getting her phone number instead. We never went on a date or anything like that, but we were phone friends. All my female friends or girlfriends were from that same area.

Things at my grandparent's house was changing too. My uncle had finally moved out and started his own little life. He was dating his high school sweetheart, and she had a niece. Naturally, I ended up dating her niece Kiki.

It wasn't anything serious. I only saw her from time to time. When she did come over, I'd go down to his house if I wasn't down there already. Even with my raging hormones, all we did was just hang out. You know, talk, a kiss here and there, and watch TV.

I also had another little friend from the same city named Janet. We met at the movies. It was my cousin, my sister's cousin, myself, and a lot of other people just hanging out one day. A group of girls was sitting behind us, and I remember climbing over the back of the chairs at the movie theater to go talk to them.

My cousin was like, "Idiot, you can just get up and walk around." But my dumb ass had to make a scene, jumping over the chairs like I didn't have any home training. Anyway, we exchanged numbers and just became really good friends.

My uncle had a vehicle, so he'd take me over

to Janet's house. Her mother was cool with males coming over and even going to her room. We never had sex or anything like that; we were just hanging out and doing what teenagers did back then.

It was crazy because Kiki was cool with Janet. They had a class together, and they knew about each other. The conversations weren't always good because they would call me at the same time to see who I was going to talk to. I didn't think anything of it; I was just having fun. I wasn't trying to be in a serious relationship back then. I was in high school, playing football, and just trying to figure out what my next move was going to be in life.

I believe my junior year was the best year ever. Just like before, I was the class clown. Benny and I had a few classes together, including the one taught by my running back coach. I remember this popular action movie had just come out, and we would act like we were dodging bullets like the main character did. I'm talking jumping on top of the teacher's desk to dance and everything.

My coach got tired of it, so he called the principal's office.

"Hey," he yelled through the intercom, "These dudes out here acting a fool. They being straight idiots." We had to go down to the office to get "paddled."

"I'm a grown-ass man," I said to Benny. "I'm not getting no paddle." Man.... The principal bent me over his desk, gave me my licks, and I went back to class like nothing happened. Everybody in the classroom knew that I had got licks because I could barely sit down. I don't think I ever acted up in his class again after that.

***

Our track team did pretty decent that year. We didn't go to state, but the boy's track team won district overall. I went to regionals in the 4 x 100 sprint relay and the 100-meter dash. It was a different feeling being on the varsity team now that I was a junior.

My first two years were more exciting because we just had the overall talent and speed. Honestly, me now being the fastest guy in our district was an eye-opener. I wish I had the ability to carry the team further than what I did, but it still turned out to be a pretty good year. We just didn't go to state. Another team ended up breaking our 4 x 100 relay team's record, and I think they won state as well. The next thing I know, school was out for the summer.

Summertime was a little different this year. I did not get a summer job, but I still had my side hustle ironing my grandfather's work clothes. Eventually, I went back to Michigan to be with my mom.

Heading back to Michigan in 2001 to see my brother graduate was a blessing in disguise. He came out of high school before me.

I remember going to his grandmother's house waiting for him to get off work, but he didn't come straight home. We waited a long time, but it was cool. I waited all those years to see him again, so a few more hours didn't hurt. I was excited inside, but I didn't show it on the outside. You know how it is... got to look hard.

Back at Mama's house, they set up a room for me to sleep in while I was visiting for the summer. The funny thing is we winded up sleeping in the same room. All we did was hang out and play video games. I forget how many people graduated with him, but it was triple my senior class.

As they were walking across the stage, I remember seeing people dancing to receive their diplomas for the first time. I'd never seen anything like that before in person or on TV.

Yeah...my brother is a special character with a unique personality. He worked at my favorite burger place around the corner from his house. When I tell you he used to hook me up, I mean I used to go there with a dollar or sometimes no money at all and come out with $10-$15 worth of food.

That's all we ever did. Go to the house, play video games, and get fat. I had a high metabolism, so I did not have to worry about getting back into football shape.

My uncle, his best friend, and my grandfather

played a tremendous role in my life up to that point, and I thank them deeply for that. But that particular summer, I finally met my father's side of the family.

One day, my brother and I were going to pick up our mother from a friend's house to take her to another friend's house who stayed on the opposite side of Michigan. Before we got to the house to pick her up, we saw a group of females hanging outside. We rode past the house and made a plan that once we picked up our mother and dropped her off, we were going to go back over there to talk to the girls. So, we picked up Mama and you'll never guess what happened.

As we were going back down the same street that we saw the girls, our Mama told us to pull in behind a car that was close to the house the girls were at. She gets out, so my brother and I start trying to spit our game.

A few moments later, a lady that stood at about 4'8 came out of the house and said, "Antoine, I'm your auntie and those are your cousins." Boy, let me tell you... My auntie was a character. She didn't care who you were, where you were from, or who you belonged to; she would cuss you out for no reason at all. My brother and I looked at each other and were in shock.

It was a little embarrassing, but it was the first time I met my favorite cousin, Peanut. I look at her like my little sister. She was skin and bones, unbelievably beautiful, and a bug-a-boo. If it were not for her, I truly do not believe that I would have got the opportunity to really meet and hang out with my father's side of the family.

She would always call the house when I was there because her aunt stayed right around the corner. Once she found that out, she would always come to the house. If I didn't pick up the phone, she knew where to find me. She was like a pest who always somehow popped up out of nowhere.

***

After my brother's graduation, I went back to Texas to finish my senior year of high school. Peanut and I's relationship grew, and we stayed in contact throughout my senior year. We were building a brother/sister relationship even though we were cousins. She didn't want anything from me except for our relationship to grow. We missed so many years out of each other's lives, and it was a blessing in disguise.

When I first met her, I didn't know what to think about it. After all, I was about to try to holler at her. I'm glad it turned out the way it did. I'd call her and check up on her from time to time, and we would talk about any and everything. We had a bond unlike anything I had with my own brother and sister.

My senior year started out with a perfect football season. We had the same schedule that we had my junior year, and we went 1-2. Before our district play jumped off, I was just starting as the running back for the varsity team.

FYI, district play comes after regular season play, in case you didn't know. As for Kai, he was on the All-American football team, and I was following his lead. It was his team because he was there longer.

Luckily, we both clicked well on the field. There was no issues on who would get the most carries. Come to find out, he had the most carries with over 1000 yards. We supported each other throughout the whole season. When he went in at running back, I would go in at the full-back position. From time to time, we were able to switch it up and switch who played what position. It was respect and love for the whole season.

We didn't have any classes together, but I know one class I was the teacher's aid. Do you know I was trying to figure out what I was going to do after I graduated high school because I didn't have a plan? Here I was in my senior year and had no clue what was next. I didn't take my schoolwork seriously, and I was doing just enough to get by. I wasn't failing any classes, but I still maintained a low B average.

Although I didn't know what was next, I was still somewhat focused. The only certain thing was that I wasn't ready to graduate high school. One interesting thing I remember is the different grading systems. We didn't have D's or E's in Texas, while in Michigan, we had everything from A-F.

We won district in our football season, which was an awesome feeling. The unthinkable happened in 2001; we lost one of our classmates. She was a cheerleader that I had a few classes with. This girl was sharp, being our valedictorian.

I remember getting up on Saturday morning, just like after any other game, and going over to my buddy's house. We were talking about the game, what I did wrong, and what I needed to focus on for the next game when he broke the news to me. "Aye, man," he said solemnly, "we lost a classmate."

I didn't believe him. I went home a few hours later, and my auntie told me the same thing. I didn't believe her either. It wasn't until I went to school on Monday that it sunk in. The whole school stopped having class that day. You could see the hurt and disbelief on everyone's faces.

I broke down inside because I had to finally face the reality that someone I saw every day was really gone. It was my first real encounter with death and the realization that tomorrow isn't promised.

I can't describe the feeling that I felt that day. By the next week, everyone had a lot of pent up anger and sadness bottled up. After the funeral service, we had football practice, and it was game on. For the lower classmen it was a regular game, but for the seniors, it was all out brawl. We went full throttle and hit every hole and knocked down everything in our way. We were practicing with a chip on our shoulders, and it showed.

We ended up making it to the second round of the playoffs, and we lost to the same team we lost to my junior year. That was the end of my high school career playing football. We played our tails off, but we just couldn't go all the way.

After that, I went to every class on time because by then, I was ready to graduate high school. Track season came and went. I actually pulled my hamstring, so I didn't even get the opportunity to compete my senior year.

I remember going to prom for the first time. Our star running back got me a date, and believe me when I say it was one to remember. She was already in college with his girlfriend, so I had bragging rights. Prior to prom, a female that I had been crushing on asked me if I wanted to go with her. The funny thing is she was dating someone else, but I guess that fell through. By the time she asked me, I already had a date.

When I told my grandmother what color my prom date was, the first thing that came out of her mouth was, "You don't have any skillets to take to the prom?"

I was like, "No, ma'am." We went to the prom together and had a good time. Afterward, we kept in contact for probably a month or so. I have not spoken to her since.

A few of my buddies told me if I would've ran track my senior year, I probably would've got a scholarship. Since I pulled my hamstring, we'll never know. I did ask the coach to call a couple of junior colleges for me so that I could try out for their football teams, but that didn't pan out. I know I didn't have the grades to get into one of the Division 1 (D1) schools because I didn't take anything seriously.

STARTING FROM SCRATCH

Life after high school got off to a slow start. I started out at the local college roughly around 15-20 miles from my house in East Texas. It was my first time away from home, and I lived in a dorm. All my classes were regular prerequisite classes.

I took an athletic class because I still wanted to try to play football, but the school didn't have a football team. All they had was basketball, baseball, and a few other sports that I didn't participate in. I tried to play baseball my senior year of high school. I went to 2 or 3 practices, but it just wasn't for me. Looking back, I think I should've put forth more effort.

The college life wasn't too bad. I was still trying to find my own way. Before college kicked off, I got a job working at the local chicken factory in the same town that the college was in. I didn't have a vehicle or even a license, so Benny drove me to and from work. He was working in that same area for a few months. Right before we graduated, he was working all the time. He would come to class sometime and go right to sleep because he just got off work and only got a couple hours to rest. Benny didn't play any other sports.

He was trying to keep his head above water, graduate, and start a new life after high school. I remember seeing the struggle in his eyes every single day. He'd come to class, and they would be bloodshot red from not getting any rest.

He really was out there just trying to provide for him and his family. That's all to say that even with all that going on, he was the one who picked me up every day and brought me home. He helped me out a lot, and I truly thank him for that.

I stopped working at the local chicken factory and focused more on school, but one thing that I didn't know was that the party life was about to find me. Thursday nights were college nights, and I had a 7 o'clock class every Friday morning. When I tell you that those nights were parties like nothing I've seen before.... I wasn't 21 yet, but somehow, I was still able to buy drinks all by myself. I would make it to class the next day and go straight to sleep.

Because it was college, the teachers didn't care if you slept. It was your money, not theirs. The only time they would wake me up is if I was snoring. Other than that, they just kept on doing their job. They weren't there to babysit or hold your hand.

I remember when we had the opportunity to practice with the girl's college basketball team to help them out for their season. I had fun doing it. We were just practicing and having a good time.

I remember having a roommate named G-Man when I was in college. He was a pretty boy and a really cool dude. He was so nice that he used to always let me play his video games. As a matter of fact, that's how I made a couple dollars every now and again. I would play video games against other people in the dorm. It was easy money, to be honest. The only thing that irked me was that he has his clothes all over the place. He had a whole bunch while I only have a couple of shirts and 2-3 pairs of pants. It was quite the experience.

I was living on my own away from home. I

tried not to depend on anybody, but when it was time for me to do my laundry, I used to call my grandmother. She would come to pick me up for the weekend and do my laundry. If I had a license, I could've driven from home to school and even put a couple dollars in my pocket.

Instead, I was a poor college student trying to figure out life. I still wanted to play football, so I hopped online and started searching for other schools. I emailed roughly 20 different junior colleges all over the states trying to find someone who would take me.

One in Illinois, replied back, and I finally had a college visit set. I had it all figured out. I'd visit my sister, who still stayed in Michigan, then chill with her for a couple weeks before I took my college visit. I had a few dollars in my pocket from when I was working at the local chicken factory. I managed to save it because I didn't know where my next paycheck was coming.

When I took the college visit, I was fat and out of shape. The coach told me that he liked the tapes I put together for him, but he was not looking for any more running backs. However, I could come to try out for the team.

The first thing that popped up in my head was all the emails that I sent him. Everything in the phone calls, conversations, and tapes centered around that position. Naturally, I was stuck on playing running back. I was pissed, to say the least. This dude made me spend all my little money. HELL, he could have saved me the trouble and told me that over the phone.

So, that fell through, along with all my dreams and hopes of playing college football. I didn't want to move back to East Texas with my grandparents because there was nothing there, so I talked to my sister about living with her on the D-block as we called it. We just had to keep everything low-key because she was on a special housing program that only allowed two people to live in the house—her and her daughter. I didn't have anywhere else to go, so it worked out for me.

I ended up enrolling in the same ju-co that my mother went to. I can remember when me and my sister were little, we used to catch the bus up there. One day while my mother was in class and taking a test, me and my sister were sitting in a corner, and I spilled some juice on the floor. Sad, sad day that was.

When I went back years later as a student myself, the whole campus had changed. I wasn't in prerequisite classes this time; I was taking the regular classes. I was having a good time enjoying life, but my sister had her rules and regulations. It was her household, and I was a guest. So, I had to listen.

While I was in school, I needed to make some money. I finally got a job at at the chicken spot a few blocks away from my sister's place. We didn't have a vehicle, so most of the time I either walked to work or our friend would drop me off and pick me up. As for living with my sister, I didn't like her rules and regulations. A lot of times, I would stay over at my auntie's house, and she would make sure I got to work. Even though I did not live with my sister 24/7, I would still give her money every now and again to help her out.

I would bounce back-and-forth from my Aunt Fefe house to my sister's house when I got bored. Hey, I had to switch things up every now and then. I was having the time of my life, but I wasn't enjoying it as much as I could because I didn't have anything going for me. I was 21 years old didn't have a car, license, or a pot to piss in.

Aunt Fefe would also take me to the other side of Michigan about two hours from her house to see my father (her brother). His wife was at work at the time when I went over there to visit him. I didn't care for going back and visiting the old neighborhood that we lived in when I was younger. I was trying to forget that lifestyle altogether.

I would go to my other auntie's house from time to time. Sometimes she'd come to pick me up, and other times, I wouldn't see her until like two weeks later.

Those were the times that I didn't really care for because people were making me do things that I didn't want to do. Just because I didn't have a place to stay didn't mean that you could treat me or talk to me in any type of way. I didn't like being taken for granted, but I understood that if it's your household, you can do whatever you want to. At the end of the day, when someone started acting funny, I'd bounce from my sister's house to my auntie's house.

Things weren't working out the way that I planned, but I still had hope. My sister and I got along pretty well for the most part. Every now and then, things got a little crazy. When I tell you we used to argue over the stupidest stuff, it was ridiculous. You name it, we argued about it. Taking out the trash, cleaning up, and a whole bunch of small stuff.

Eventually, I talked to my Aunt Roro, who stayed in Louisiana and moved back to the south to live with her and her family. This is the same aunt that had the two boys that I was always doing the chores for. It seemed like a good idea at the time. *That* was one of the craziest decisions that I've ever made, but I had to move out there. I was trying to find myself, and living inside that household with my auntie was not for me.

MILITARY LIFE

By the end of 2002, I was still trying to figure things out. I didn't have my shit together. All I knew was that I was just tired of people taking the keys away from me to their household for things that I didn't have anything to do with. My grandmother would get mad at my auntie and take her key. My auntie would get mad at my grandmother and take her keys away from me.

As for me, I was shitless, not homeless. I had to play both sides in order for me to have somewhere to lay my head at night. I was stuck in the middle of a childish situation between a mother and a daughter, but what could I do? Hell, I was 21 years old and did not have a car or a license. All I could do was go with the flow.

Before everything started happening between my grandmother and her daughter, I was still living with my auntie in Louisiana with her and her two boys. I was working this odd job after school and on the weekends. I was getting paid weekly—one week from the tip pool, which was cash from busting tables, and the other from my actual paycheck. I would have to give my auntie and uncle money for rent and also buy little items around the house like toilet paper, paper towels, soap, and laundry detergent.

While I was doing all that, I was also going to college. I started off really well, maintaining a 4.0 GPA. Somewhere along the line between me bouncing from Texas to Michigan and Louisiana, I was holding on to a 2.0. I loved going to school and working because I didn't like being at that chaotic house. I needed my own space, and I was fed up with depending on somebody else to pick me up from work and school.

When my auntie and I had our fallouts, I would have to call somebody to help me out. Mind you, I didn't have a lot of friends to depend on. She would always tell me to figure out the bus schedule. Even after I put gas in the car and purchased 2-4 boxes of cigarettes for her, she would tell me something like that. That wasn't part of the deal, but she'd get mad if I didn't do it. I was thumbing and bombing my way from school and work. I had to catch a ride here, there, or wherever I could.

The day I ran into a recruiter in the hallway at college was a blessing in disguise. He was recruiting for the Army reserve, and he took me down to the recruiting station to do my paperwork. I redid the test, and the scores were pretty low, so I was under the impression that I would have to retake the Army test to get in.

The reserve recruiter left, and I found myself talking to the active duty recruiter who put soldiers in the Army. We talked for roughly 30 minutes before she said, "Antoine, you don't have a car. You don't have a place to stay. So, you're going to sign this paperwork." I listened to her, and I never look back.

When I shipped off to basic training on October 28, 2004, I did not know what I was getting myself into. The paperwork said 11 x-ray. I had no idea what that was. I didn't Google or do any research on it either.

I was just happy to leave the house and be out on my own for the second time. The only difference was that I couldn't call my grandparents to come pick me up. I was on my way to Georgia, the home of the infantryman. This was my first time on a plane to anywhere. I had traveled before, but it was by bus or car with my grandfather.

When I got to Georgia, we did all the normal processes. We got our medical briefs, finances, and our clothes before getting ready to start basic training. I thought basic training was going to be the same as the processing center. Surprisingly, it was more relaxed.

We went to the DFAC and got to eat whatever we wanted. I was able to get 2-3 servings of ice cream. As a matter of fact, I got all the seconds and thirds that I wanted. I was living my fat-boy dreams.

So, there it was, like heaven in disguise. I was so happy. I was getting paid three hots and a cot, and I didn't have to worry about nobody yelling or fussing. I was so excited.

Hell, I told myself I should've joined the Army many years ago like my little brother did. He joined as a supply specialist, and I followed in his footsteps after my first deployment... we can talk about that piece later. Boy, was I happy. I was in for a rude awakening.

I can't recall the date, but I remember we had to go outside with all our bags and gear to wait to get picked up to go to the basic training area. At the time, I didn't know about the buses that picked us up.

Come to find out, they were called cattle buses. The seats were limited, and it was a big open area to put the soldiers in. They call it butt to nut because they were adding so many people into one vehicle. I tried not to let it get under my skin. I was just sitting on my bags and wondering what the next step was going to be in my journey. All I knew was that I was going to go down range to basic training to learn how to shoot, move, communicate, and kill. That's all.

To pass time, I got up to walk around, and someone called me out. "That's Kincaid right there," the guy said proudly. "When he gets downrange, they're going to call him Killa K." The other guys agreed and starting to gas my head up. I was so excited to have a new nickname that I couldn't stop smiling.

"Hell, yeah!" I shouted. "Let's do this."
It was a bunch of us sitting outside, just relaxing and waiting on the cattle bus to pick us up. After another hour or so, about six or seven cattle buses came in front of us. I was super excited.

It was finally time. A dude with a round and brown drill sergeant hat on was screaming and yelling at us. The cattle buses didn't even come to a complete stop before they were jumping off to get in our faces.

"Get down!"
"Get up!
"Hurry up!"

I looked to my left, then to my right, and wondered what I got myself into. I was nervous. Hell, we all were nervous and scared. I wondered what happened to everybody being nice. Once we jumped on the bus, everyone started pushing and yelling at each other to find space, I had three bags while everybody else had way more. I almost pissed myself I was so scared. I heard somebody say it's going to be okay, but I still couldn't relax. It was a day I will never forget.

The first few nights, we didn't go to bed till about 2200-2300 because they had to teach us how to fix our lockers, beds, and all our paperwork was in order. I remember they used to come in the middle of the night and just mess with us for no reason. Basically, they were trying to adapt us from a civilian life to military life.

The move down range to basic training was a nightmare, but it was good for my soul. We trained hard, woke up at all types in the morning, and learned discipline. If the drill sergeants weren't messing with us, then we were busy doing some hands-on training. Those first eight weeks was all about getting into shape and preparing our minds for Advanced Individual Training (AIT).

Taking a shower for the first few nights was crazy because lights out was at 2200, and we have 55 personnel who had to take a shower. Also, we have to make sure that the common areas were clean after everyone was done. For the first few nights, our plan was to use the sinks to wash up. When we got in the shower, we just rinsed off the soap. That way, our showers were approximately two minutes long per person. The last few would have to clean up behind us. To keep things fair, we rotated every night.

I also met one of my close friends during this time named Martin. He's like a brother to me, and we still communicate to this day. We were in a front leaning rest, which is like a push-up position, together in basic training. It was at this point that I got my second nickname: Doughboy.

I went to basic training weighing in at 210 pounds. When I left basic training, I was 176 pounds. My buddy Martin found all the weight that I lost. He came into basic weighing about 130 pounds and left weighing about 160. All the weight that I lost my body gained in muscle.

As for my friend, he and I became close friends; we really motivated each other to make it through basic training. We were like Beavis and Butthead. We would go to the range, and he would outshoot me. Half the time, I did not qualify until he qualified. It was like I was following him the whole way.

After a few weeks, we had a Christmas Exodus break. Since Georgia wasn't too far from Louisiana, I decided to take the bus home. I didn't feel like flying. I remember as we were marching to the bus stop to get dropped off at the bus station, we were in our Class A uniforms marching in sync, but we didn't sound off loud enough for the drill sergeant's liking. As a result, he put us in a front leaning rest position. I was shocked.

"Drill sergeant," I said hesitantly, "I just got the uniform out the cleaners." Little did I know, I made it worse. We did a bunch of push-ups then we went to the position of attention. After that, we did a right face and sounded off as loud as ever, to his liking. It sucked because I was standing there in my uniform all sweaty in the middle of December. Another lesson learned: don't question authority. Ever.

***

I can recall our first field exercise before

we went on leave. It was cold outside, and my buddy Mike with his dumb ass had the bright idea to not sleep in his sleeping bag. "I'm not gonna pull out my sleeping bag," he said proudly, "I'm just sleeping in my chemical suit." It was thick, but he should have known that it wasn't going to be thick enough.

Around 10 o'clock at night, he woke me up all frantic. "Kincaid! Kincaid! Can you help me, man?" he said as his teeth were practically chattering. "I need to find my sleeping bag. I'm cold, man."

I did help him out, but I was talking about him the whole time. We didn't have a tent or anything; we actually were just sleeping outside on the ground under the stars. Yeah, it was a little uncomfortable, but we didn't mind because all the training that we did prepared us for it. Honestly, we were just so excited about sleeping for a few hours.

That week had been tiresome, and we were drained. Even though we had to train in the field, we still had fireguard duty. When it was my turn, I woke up my buddy and told him I'd pay him $40 to pull my shift. He hit me with a hell no, so I had to work. I was so tired that night.

When we woke up the next day, we packed our gear and got ready for the day. After breakfast, we was getting smoked. I'm talking about being completely worn out like it was no tomorrow. The drill sergeant said it was to warm us up, and I was so cold I'd do anything at that moment.

Basic training had its ups and downs. It wasn't bad, but I was worried because I didn't know what I was getting myself into. Everything you can think of we did.

I remember using the bugle sticks and getting my ass whooped. We went to the range and marched with all our gear. It truly was an awesome experience, and I'm glad I had the opportunity to go to that basic training. I wouldn't have done it any other way.

Since we were 11 x-rays becoming 11 bravos, we did our AIT in the same spot. We were in the same platoon, and the same bed. We woke up, and a drill sergeant said, "Welcome to AIT."

It was gruesome. We knocked out a couple of push-ups, did personal hygiene, and got ready for the day. We only had the opportunity to take one pass at a time. Think of the pass like a hall pass in school that allows you to do certain things. Since I failed my PT test, I had to go along with the other drill sergeant, and I didn't' get a pass. I couldn't go with my battle buddy, but I still had the opportunity to take advantage of getting my haircut, making personal phone calls, and eating whatever. I just couldn't do it with my battle buddies.

We only had three hours to do everything. After that, we'd march right back to our barracks.

***

The day before graduation, my sister, auntie, cousin, and my sister's friend came down to Georgia. We had the opportunity of going out to eat together before I was shipped off to my next duty station in Washington.

More than half our company in basic training was shipped off to this place in Washington. During the plane ride, I was a nervous wreck. My buddy Mike, the same idiot that said he was going to sleep in his chemical suit became my roommate in Washington.

Once I got to Washington, we had to go to replacement, which is like a reception. Luckily, somebody was there to receive us. After spending a week or so at replacement and in processing, I finally got the opportunity to go to my unit.

It was set in a classroom environment with all the desks facing the front. All the soldiers that were getting off the bus had to go into that particular classroom. I remember this bald head man who had dip in his mouth was asking those random questions about the Army and how much knowledge that we had gained from basic training. I didn't know that he was handpicking who he wanted. He picked myself and a few other guys to be a part of his company.

We were placed in groups alphabetically, so my buddy Mike was in a different group.

Once I got assigned a room, this time, I picked the bottom bunk. During basic training, I was usually on the top bunk, and I was always afraid that I was going to fall off. Also, when my brother came to stay the night, I always slept on the bottom bunk as well. Having the opportunity to pick the bottom bunk was the highlight of my day.

Once I got settled in, I still didn't have any linen. When I saw my buddy getting off the bus, it was his turn to go inside the classroom and talk to the bald-headed man. Come to find out, he was our first sergeant. He picked my buddy to join his organization as well. I didn't know at first that my buddy played a trick on me. He told me he was going to be put in the same company, but we're not roommates.

I said, "Shit, man. It's cool because we can still communicate with each other."

A couple of seconds later, he said, "Man, I'm bullshitting with you. We're roommates."

Who knew that the dude that I met in basic training was going to be like my brother. We were some of the first soldiers because there was not a lot of NCOs in the company. The unit was brand new starting from scratch, so it was a big ole gaggle fuck for PT in the morning.

A few weeks went by, and that's when we started getting more soldiers and NCOs. We finally were starting to become a unit. We still didn't have any equipment, so we had to borrow equipment from different organizations. Another thing we'd do is go sign out some rubber ducky's and conducted our training. Rubber duckies were like plastic weapons we could use for training purposes. Hey, we had to do what we had to do.

During training, we walked everywhere—the range, the shoot house, etc. The only vehicle that we had at the time was the supply vehicle. I didn't know what the supply room was because I was going to the PX to buy my own supplies. The PX is like a Walmart on post. Someone told me later on that I was wrong and to go down to the supply room to get whatever I needed. If it wasn't there, then that damn supply sergeant had better order it, or go get it, whichever came first.

There was no equipment to train with, but we always conducted PT in the morning and again in the afternoon. I wasn't a good runner at the time. I failed my PT in basic training, and when I got to my unit, I was still having a hard time with my run. My runtime went from barely passing to running a 13:23, which was a pretty decent run to me. There were others in the platoon who were like gazelles.

***

My roommate was unpredictable. One day, my roommate made a joke about me that I didn't like at all. It's so bad that I don't even want to repeat it. The bottom line is we had a 10-second little argument, but we didn't speak to each other for a few days. What made us end up talking again was when I hit my head on the cabinet where I kept my cleaning supplies and toiletries. He made a joke about it, and it was just like old times.

Every Thursday we ordered three pizzas for

$5 each from the pizza place up the road. We each would have one to ourselves then split the other one down the middle. We had a good little system going with those Thursday pizza runs.

***

Once we started again with the equipment, I became the company armor, which learns how to take weapons apart and put them back together again. If something was broken at my particular level that I can fix, I'd fix it with no problem. Now, if you asked me how to fix a weapon now, I wouldn't be much help because I'm a bit rusty.

Martin and I were in the same platoon and the same squad. Since I didn't have my driver's license at the time, I was put into weapon squad as the 240 bravo machine gunner. I held every position in weapon squad, and my buddy was the RTO. Everything that we did, we did at the same time. We practically did everything together.

He ended up getting married and going to another company to become a sniper. I had the opportunity of trying out as well, but I turned it down because I was told by my squad leader that I was getting ready to go to the promotion board.

He said if I stayed there, I'd become a noncommissioned officer. The only thing I needed to work on was my voice because I was soft-spoken. I'm still soft spoken, and I'm shy at times. Come to find out, I never went to the board in that unit. The only thing I did was my job.

***

At some point, I met a woman on social media named Kat, who I fell in love with. We ended up getting married prior to my first deployment to Iraq in 2007. The weapon squad trained with different squads in the platoon. We were learning their language and how to use it in combat.

We made it to Kuwait Easter Sunday night of 2007. It was hot out and sweaty in the house at night.

I remember flying into Iraq in the middle of

the night. I gave up my spot so that somebody else could take my spot. You know the Army is bigger than Specialist Kincaid

When I finally made it in, they told me to just pick a spot, get some Racktime, and I'd find my squad in the morning. The whole company was inside this building, configured like a warehouse. There were no individual rooms; just a bunch of cots where everybody was located at.

After training and getting used to the time zone and temperature in Iraq, we got the word that we was about to go into the city and start working. Everything that we've trained on for the past two years was about to happen. We were about to go fucking do it.

I remember our first sergeant said, "We killed the dumb ones years ago. These are the smart ones. Now. They think outside the box, so nothing but headshots."

Man, that little speech right there got everyone's morale up. I remember before we left for Iraq, we were still back in Washington when our company commander made a speech. He said, "Look to your left. Look to the right. Everybody's not coming back. A few tears dropped inside my soul."

"Is that true?" I asked my squad leader.

"Yeah, it is. It is in our job description."

At that moment, I tried to think about my whole life. I tried to re-play my whole life right then and there. I looked from left to right. I was speechless.

***

2007: The first day I put my boots on ground in a combat zone in Iraq. To give you an idea of how it all worked, as a gunner, you're always attached to a particular squad with each mission along with someone like me. It was my first mission, and I was attached to second squad. Not my gunner, just me by myself. I was nervous and scared shitless; it was a lot different than training.

We had a system where everybody could talk and see each other. One of the team leaders was telling me to come here, and I couldn't see the gear. It was just a bunch of madness cause I was sweating, and it was getting in my eyes so much that I had to take off my eye pro just to see. All this was happening at night, and I was freaking out. We went inside a place called the tree line, and I was the last soldier so I had to take a few paces back to watch the rear. The soldier in front of me was like, "I got you. Just follow in my footsteps." Clearly he could tell how nervous I was.

"Roger. I gotcha."

Well, it turned out to be a mess following his footsteps. I fell in some mud mixed with something that wreaked of animal droppings, and my whole weapon got covered with the stench also. Once we got through, I was muddy from head to toe.

We were only supposed to be out there for 2-3 days, and that turned into two weeks. I didn't have a uniform to change into, and it was just a bunch of mess. So, I had to wash my clothes inside a mop bucket and let it hang dry outside. Literally 30 minutes later, it was dry. Yes, it was that hot in Iraq.

21 May 2007: We had our mission, but our mission didn't go as planned. Nothing bad on our part; we conducted our mission, but our commander thought that we should've been out there a little longer. I remember him just yelling and fussing and cussing, so we had to fill up sandbags for hours. It was fun because our whole platoon was together.

Right after that, we had to go on guard. We had to get up and get ready to go on R&R soon. We were excited but disappointed at the same time because we were only deployed for a few months. We wanted to go home like midway through our deployment to give our families and friends enough time to miss us.

I remember getting our mission brief and going to sleep, then waking up at around 3 o'clock in the morning. I was getting ready to go out, and I saw Sergeant Town. go into the freezer and grab some ice and put it in his camelbak. Damn, that's a good idea, I said to myself. So, I did the same thing and grabbed a couple of ice cubes to put in my camelbak. We didn't know how long it was going to take us to get back to get ready to clean our weapons.

During the mission, I was on the south side of the road with the same idiot that told me to follow in his footsteps when I fell in the mud on May 5. It was my first time leading the squad. Our platoon Sergeant had a team on the north side of the road and was clearing the route for the vehicles to come through. That morning I did something that I'd only ever done in training. Only this time.... it wasn't at target. It was a white vehicle.

Somebody must have been saying a prayer for him because not one bullet hit him. He got hit by a piece of glass from the window. He stopped, threw a cigarette out on the ground, and let them search and secure him. They gave him first aid and an omelet MRE. That was crazy. Back in the Stryker, we talked about it for a while, and then we continued with the mission.

This was one of my worst days in Iraq. My

best man came out the Stryker vehicle and said Sergeant Town was dead. I had to check for myself. I didn't believe him, so I put my head inside their vehicle and sure shit you, I've never seen anything like that before. It was like a scene from a movie.

***

Later on that year, I would run into Mike again. He was in the same battalion but just a different company. We talked about our future in the Army, and I told him I was going to get out. He talked me into re-classing. We talked and joked for a couple minutes then went to the MWR because he had something to show me.

Come to find out, he didn't know how to tell me that Kat was on the internet hooking up with another dude. I was shocked because I talked to this woman not every day but at least once or twice a week. The city that we were living in in Iraq only had one computer for the whole company to use. We also only had one satellite phone for the whole company to use when we were out on a mission.

When I got back, I wasn't thinking about no phone or computer. I just wanted to get some shut eye and some chow. I wasn't thinking about making any phone calls or emailing when it wasn't no holiday coming up. I had just seen her a few months earlier because of R&R, so I couldn't believe it.

If one thing that hurt my soul, it was the fact that I was across the country not knowing if I was going to come back or not...yet, I was paying all the bills and making sure she was straight. It hurt, but I didn't want to give up on us. I looked at it is as we were just going through stuff and could still fix things up. Well, at least I thought we did when I made it back from Iraq.

***

My buddy talked me into re-classing to work in supply. I did it, and when I made it back from Iraq, I finally went to school for supply. It was a different type of experience, but I had fun.

My first deployment we lost some damn

good leaders. Rest easy, my brothers.... rest easy.

***

I wasn't used to working with any females inside the Army besides the ones that we had attached to the squad when we went out on a mission in Iraq. This was different. I had to change my language a lot because being a part of 11 Bravo...well... let's just say our language is not PG. It was the way of the world at that time.

The complacency level and discipline level is totally different from combat arms to support. It was a lot more camaraderie being in combat arms. Being support... I haven't seen it yet. It was so strange because I didn't see that being in combat arms. I don't know if my eyeballs were shut tight or what, but I never saw that.

It's a different Army world than what I was used to. I had to use more of my brain because I was just so used to shooting, moving, communicating, then killing. That was the gist of working in combat arms.

Now, I have to do paperwork which I wasn't used to. I did some paperwork when I used to work for the company armor, but those skills came overtime.

Eventually, I did learn the process and made a bunch of mistakes. I was ordering the wrong weapon parts more than one time, keeping a weapon out the fight for multiple weeks because I ordered the wrong part, and all kinds of stuff.

I never saw a tent until I worked support. I still remember the first time I heard my commander say, "Aye, make sure we have the tent ready so that we can set up the training room."

I said straight up, "Well, ma'am, I'm used to sleeping up under the stars with my sleeping bag. Half the time, I didn't get my sleeping bag because we were that tired. I always kept my woobie aka blanket in my poncho liner that I carried in my assault pack. It was just easier for me to get to when we was out there training."

When I was combat arms, it was a must to

carry it like that. I would have lots of Ziploc bags with my socks, t-shirts, underclothes, etc. Then, in my side pouches, I'd have my woobie. The whole idea of using a tent was definitely a different change of pace as well.

After finishing my AIT training to become a Supply Specialist, I got an assignment to Texas. I was excited because I would get to see my wife a lot more. At the time, we were in the process of purchasing our first home.

Now, you've read my life story. I never thought in a million years that someone like me, coming from the background that I came from will be able to purchase a home at the age of 26. She and I talked about moving to Texas to get us a fresh start in life because of what she had done in the past, so we were very excited to start new.

I was only five hours away from East Texas. Even though I was right around the corner, I went home every blue moon. Honestly, I didn't take the opportunity as I should have to go home, but I still went home every now and again. And when I did go, it usually wasn't planned.

Sometimes, I'd just leave. I didn't have a pass or leave form signed. If it was nothing on the training calendar, a four-day weekend, or I wasn't on duty, I'd just get in my car and drive home. For some reason, my wife didn't make the trip with me. I never asked why... I just got in my car and drove off.

***

2011 was my second deployment to Iraq. It was totally different than the first time. I lived in a chu, which was just a container with windows and a door. It looked kind of like a smart home. I spent more than half the deployment in there by myself.

Towards the end of our deployment, I moved in with my buddy Mitch to share a chu because we were closing down in Iraq. It was around the time when a well-known comedian dropped a popular stand up. I would just have my headphones on, laughing and irritating my buddy when he was trying to get some sleep. I would be over there just giggling and talking to myself nonstop to make sure he heard me.

When he used to get around other people, he'd talk nothing but shit. Therefore, I had to return the favor by annoying him every chance I got while we were in the chu. It was all in good fun. Despite us picking on each other, he was a great mentor.

He actually lived within walking distance of my new house I had in Texas. Our wives took turns dropping us off and picking us up from clubs and bars.

This one particular time, we both got shitfaced at this club after his wife dropped us off. If you name it, we were drinking it. I'm talking about knocking them back left and right. My wife picked us up later that night, and the conversation that we had the next day was crazy. I didn't remember a thing, but apparently I told her that we were a mile from the house, but when she picked us up, we were outside the club. Good times...good times.

***

At work, I was a staff sergeant. People called me a baby staff sergeant because I was by rank the newest staff sergeant in the platoon. Our platoon sergeant had left to go to his next assignment, and I became the new platoon sergeant.

As you can imagine, there were some people who didn't agree with that decision made by the 1SG. They asked my predecessor stuff like, "Why is he the platoon sergeant when he's just a baby staff sergeant," and "We have other staff sergeants that have been here longer than him."

My buddy didn't trip about it like some of the other guys did. He would talk shit, but at the same token, he would help me if I had any problems with anybody in the platoon.

Even though he outranked me, he would take my soldiers if needed to lighten my load or pull them off to the side and talk to them if they gave me problems. He would also say the same thing about me. "Give this idiot the opportunity. He is learning, and I am grooming him to become a great leader."

Like I said, a great mentor but also an asshole when he wanted to be. One morning for accountability formation right before PT, I didn't see my buddy anywhere. I did my usual and gave my report, which is like a roll call. Since I didn't see him, I said, "Sgt. First Class Mitch is out of ranks."

Suddenly, my whole platoon started laughing. Come to find out, he was in the building the whole time, on an assigned detail which I wasn't tracking. Later on that day, he and I got into a big argument in the hallway.

"I'm your platoon sergeant!" I yelled. "And you're going to listen to me!"

Let me tell you about Mitch. He stood about 5'6, 200 pounds. He thought he was the tallest and the strongest character on the planet, but I called him Fatboy. He was a little short, stocky fat guy—always talking about his arms and his chest. He said something like, "Aye, man, I can bench-press your house. I can pick your car up..." Blah. Blah. Blah. He would make me do push-ups because he outranked me, but it was all fun and games. He was always talking shit, but this time, we had a big falling out because of it.

Later on that day, I heard somebody on the bike in my driveway. *Who the hell is this,* I remember thinking to myself. It was him with a six-pack. That was his way of apologizing. We talked about it, and all I know is that the six-pack turned into us playing dominoes and drinking more than a couple beers.

His wife had to come pick him up from the house. We were just having a good ol' time. Funny thing is he never said, "Aye, man, I'm sorry." There was none of that. We were just drinking and talking shit. That is what we did every other week. I was either down to his house, or he was down to my house just having a good time.

***

In 2012, I received a phone call that my uncle had passed away. It was the same uncle who had pressured me into playing football. I was in shock. It really bothered me when I went home for the holidays, particularly Thanksgiving. It was just an empty space at the table with all the family there minus him.

If somebody else asked me about him, I'd always say he was on vacation. I didn't dig into it. Regardless, though, that was my uncle. If it wasn't for him, I just would've been another regular dude in high school wondering my what-ifs.

Around that same time, our company lost one of our good soldiers. He was riding his motorcycle when he got into an accident and passed away. The unit was in shock because he was the life of the company. He was the first one that told me I was getting promoted to staff sergeant.

I remember it like it was yesterday. I hadn't gone on the promotion website, and I was going to work as usual. I woke up and did my normal routine, and he and I was doing PT. Suddenly, he punched me dead in the chest.

"What the fuck you doing?" I yelled.
All he could do was smile. He told me to think about it, and I thought about it and was like, "Man, you joking."

"Nope. Congratulations."

We used to go to his house from time to time before we deployed to play spades and dominoes. It was nice to just get away from everything. You know I miss you, Boy Boy. RIP.

***

It was time for me to leave the unit, so I talked to my branch manager and got an assignment on post in a different unit. Doing that restarted my time. I had just purchased a home in May, and Kat and I were still trying to figure things out with each other. We had a son, so we were trying to keep things together to raise him. Once we got over the hump, everything should have been okay. As for my buddy, he got stationed somewhere else.

Once he left, I hung out with the neighbor Matt a few times, but it wasn't the same. With me and my buddy, we didn't have to really say who was going to do this or that. It was just natural with us. With Matt, it was a different vibe. He wasn't a bad guy or anything like that, but we just didn't connect like me and my buddy.

Regardless, though, hanging out with him was a great way to get out the house and get away from our wives. Matt and I just used to go out and just try to have fun. I knew that they were having issues when one night we were supposed to be out and instead we were facing the door of the club watching his wife...

***

Fast forward to 2014, and I found out that the children my wife and I had weren't mine. Apparently she couldn't keep her legs closed while I was out serving my country. It was time to finally call it quits. Luckily, she didn't fight for anything.

It got to the point that even my family tried to help out. My sister tried to hook me up with one of her friends, but her friend stayed in Louisiana and was always having issues.

For instance, she couldn't meet me in Texas because her tires were bad. I offered to pay for her tires, but she turned that down. I went to her city after I had surgery on my left foot, and she asked me to go with her to the club. I couldn't go because you know I was in a cast, so she was supposed to meet me at my sister's boyfriend's house the next day. She never showed up, so I said fuck it and went back to doing what I was doing.

There was one female I thought was the one. We dated roughly 3-4 years before I proposed to her. She gave me the ring back when I went to PCS. When I went to Korea, we reconnected for a short bit. I left, and she ended up getting pregnant by someone else...the rest was history.

***

I winded up going back to school after I got my associate's degree when I was in Korea. A person like me never thought that I would be getting an associate's degree, but I got it. About a week after I finished my last class, I signed up to get my bachelor's degree.

Those classes were fast and furious—each one was five weeks long with a 10-page paper as a final. I hated writing anything with school because of my dyslexia, but I didn't let that stop me.

I had a few bumps in the road on the journey to getting my degree. At one point my GPA dropped below a 2.0 when I was getting my associates, but I'm not a failure. I didn't give up on myself, and I continued to fight and go to school.

It was frustrating at times, but I continued to do what I had to do.

During that time, I was always in the house. I stayed on the phone with my sister asking her how to do this and that. I was emailing my instructors left and right because I couldn't afford to pay $750 for a class. My goal was not to fail and to keep my GPA up.

The beginning of June 2019 was an awesome year for me. I finished my last class and finally received my bachelor's degree, which I can attribute much of that to my sister.

She is so smart and played the role of peer reviewer throughout my entire bachelor's program. The joke is she has three bachelor's degrees, two with her name on it and one with mine. She was there to assist me with brainstorming, writing, editing, you name it, she was there.

I was so excited when I got promoted to Sergeant first class June 2019. Shortly after that, my buddy (Mitch) called me, and we were joking around on the phone as usual. SFC Mitch was now Mr. Mitch. He retired from the military a few years back. He was messing with me saying, "Hey first sergeant get up. Wake up, man, you got soldiers to train."

I told him, "Look, fat boy, I'm sleep. I got duty." I was acting 1SG at the time.

Little did I know, that would be my last time hearing his voice. I got off duty, made it home, and received a phone call from his wife that he was gone. I didn't believe it. My mouth dropped. I was in shock and didn't say anything for a few minutes. What could I say? I didn't know what or how to feel. All I knew is I was in shock.

I caught up with our other two buddies that we hung out with we talk shit with when we were stationed together in Texas. I thought that his wife was playing a joke because they were mad at each other. I thought 1,000 different things, but I didn't want to believe that he was gone.

Three people had to verify it before I believed it. I thought his wife was full of shit. My buddy, who was stationed in Japan at the time, confirmed it. I thought she was full of shit too. Pretty much, I thought everybody was full of shit...but I was just in denial.

When he left, he created an empty space in my heart. I don't have too many friends. I don't mess with too many people. He was the only person that I really talked to. He wouldn't judge me... he would only tell me the truth. He would tell me the truth...even if I was full of shit. He let it be known exactly what was and what wasn't. I will always carry a piece of him in my spirit.

Looking back at my life and looking at where I am now, I wouldn't change anything. You have to play the cards that you're dealt. There are many obstacles that may come in your way, and it's totally up to you how you decide to play your cards to get over them. You can make excuses, or you can play to win. This journey called life is written with our own notepads, and we decide our ending.

People, enjoy your life. Life is too short. If you have a learning disability, do not let that stop you. Continue to dream a dream. I honestly believe a person without a dream is just a walking skeleton. I could've easily made excuses and given up on myself, but I didn't. People that you choose to surround yourself with play a role in your journey, so choose wisely.

Uncle Steve been a fan for many many years. Please take the opportunity to read my first book. Please leave a review at AntoineLEF@hotmail.com

Made in the USA
Monee, IL
24 February 2021